Respectfully dedicated:

To the greatest teacher I ever had the opportunity to learn from;

LIFE

Special dedication and thanks to you, P.Y.T. (TC)

For showing me, that it's okay to love freely....

All poems and photos by;
Caros R. Pendleton

Copy right 2005

ISBN: 978-0-6151-6850-0

Table of content

Introduction	2-3
Quest of Essence	4
Angel	5
Cloudy Eyes	6
Over Stand	7
My Heart	8
Insight	9
Give Me Your Tears	10
Miss Shadow	11
In Time (Miss Shadow Part 2)	12
Once in a Life Time	13
Artistry	14
The Experience	15
A Granted Wish	17
What I Want	18
Renewed Vows	19
In My World	20
Give Me Kisses	21
Patience	22
Decisions	24
The Love Letter	25-27
I Ask You….	29
A Piece of Love…..	30
For You…	31
Because I'm,	32
Forever….	33
My Daughter	34
Until the End of Time	36
Because,	37
Insight	38
A Poem to the World	39
Be Strong My Friend	40
Lady Bug	42
Caribbean Eyes	43
Passion for Her	44
Your Choice	45
Journey	46
You Decide: A Conversation, between friends.	48-51
Insight	52
Through My Eyes	54
10 Things I Did to Break Your Heart	55
Untitled	56
One Thing I…	57
Cheating	58
Untitled	60
HER	61
From One to Another	63
The world is…	64
That Feeling	65
She…	66

Through My Eyes (part II)	67
?	68
Flame	70
Star Gazing (Dedication to a friend)	71
As We Lay	73
Injected	74
Your Touch	75
A Whole Half	76
Tears	77
Sleepless Nights	78
Untitled	79
The Question	80
Now I Know Love	81
Is It Possible?	82
Forgiveness	83
Closed Eyes/Time to Fly	85
Rainy Days	86
Distant Lover	87
EVOL	88
Join Love	89
Sunflower	90
Fate	92
Is IT Possible? (Part 2)	93
Reality	94
Soaring Angel/Once Fallen	96
Insight	97
The Exit	98
Wishful Thinking	100
Solid Confusion	101
The Beauty Darkness Brings	102
A Letter Not a Poem	103-104
While I'm down...	105
Authors Image	107

Introduction

In creating this book of poetry my objective was to create something that any one person on the face of this earth; of any race, culture or in any language can pick up and find a comfort zone within one's self, about a given situation that maybe or may have been.

Throughout my life time I have been blessed to encounter many wonderful individuals. Some which touched my soul with a glance, others who have left me with heart felt suspicions. These encounters in addition to touching me soulfully also paved a way for me to explore my inner most values and emotions.

Though many of my relationships have been a party mix of expressions, they have also played a part in me finding the true self inside. This gave me the opportunity to embark on a journey, which allowed many questions with very few answers. That has ultimately led me to a stream of divine conception. This has allowed me to indulge in everything that is pure in life, along with the gift to share it. To share love visually as it is also plain, black, white and mentally colorful.

I have found there are many different directions that poetry may take its reader. Subsequently finding them a place and an identity, which may substitute as a bridge to their emotions?

"My Relationship with Poetry" may be used as a tool to repair one's emotions in any sense of repairing something that can never be touched physically, only felt emotionally. It may also be used for the purpose of actually being able to see an emotion and or actually touching an emotion visually. "My

Relationship with Poetry", cordially takes its reader through intimate details of my life, which has created my unstable, yet firm relationship with poetry. Experiencing any relationship in its fullness is to experience your self in your most naked form. Pure, comfortable, and peaceful as all your relations should be. As if…poetry.

Quest of Essence

A woman's essence is the essence of love
It can be as sweet as sugar
Even as precious as a dove
It may be as difficult as crossing a thorn bush
Mysterious as the thickened fog
But for some reason
I must continue to push-on
In the darkness
In search of a sweetened tongue
I'm on a quest of no promised destination
So with the guidance of the man or perhaps the woman above
I search
I seek
For my Essence
My Love…

Angel

Reaching out for your aura
Your fragrance glides through my fingertips
Hoping the wind blows my way
I contemplate the direction of nature
Playing God for your…
Lust, love and emotions
Like dolphins swimming blind
I'm guided by the pulsation within your ocean
As I tiptoe on cotton
Entering and locking the door behind
Your heart is as big as I imagined

Cloudy Eyes

Look into my eyes at a glance
And clouds you may see
Look a second time with patience
And a sun that never stops shinning
Shall be revealed beyond those clouds

Over Stand

Tears in your eyes
A frown on your face
What may I do to erase
Running for resolve
I stumble over problematic
Lifted up by faith
Handed a flower from grace
I turn
I kneel
I listen
I over stand

My Heart
Out of sync, But in touch

"LOVE ONE MORE PERSON, EACH DAY EVERYDAY."

Give Me Your Tears

Give me your tears
I'll take them with joy
Rest your frown on my pillow
Fill the creases
With oceans of explored fears
Give me your tears
In my heart they'll sit
Frozen in time
Dangling from threads of purity
Give me your tears
Let me count them one by one
Give me your tears
I'll take them until there are none

Miss Shadow

She dwells among us
Going unnoticed…
'Till now.
Walking alone in the darkness
Has pushed me into the path
Of the shadow.
Hidden Interest
Secret Glances
Put away due to circumstances
Private thoughts of endless fantasies
Would be revealed
If only…
A conversation
Words spoken soft
Like the whisper of the wind
I close my eyes to imagine
…the motions of the waves
As gentle as a lions roar
Controlling yet subtle…subdued.
Like the tide
I feel drawn to her thirst for the unknown
A change from the strains of a lost love
Her embrace through the night
…Innocent
No longer the shadow
I awaken to find the silence that follows
The storm
 Untouched
By a single drop of rain…

In Time
(Miss Shadow Part 2)

Soft as rose petals
I feel her lips caress my neck
As if a butterfly
The fragility of my character
Allows a gentle stroke
To persist 'til it reaches my finger tips
Sounds of anticipation escape
To refill the silent void that has fallen upon the two us
Gently, fingertips find openings
That leads to sensations of
Unimaginable pleasure
Recollections of the shadow and her
Innocent embrace
Shall I dare Imagine?
What will come?
….In time

Once in a Life Time

I yearn for those eyes of yours
To be present with my morning yawn
As we slept well pass the breach of dawn
Warm air freshly brewed
From you to my neck
My tongue to your ear
Pulling you closer
Distance the only fear
Wanting to give you
The strength to persevere
Pondering
Wondering
If true happiness comes twice
In one year

Artistry

*Like two paintbrushes
Commencing onto one canvas
The Idea beautiful
The objective difficult
Separate Idea's of satisfaction
With one goal of passion
Creating a master piece
From two minds in sync
Patience in detail
As my princess removes her veil
No more missing links
No more wondering what my other half thinks
Soul now at peace
As we link
To create this master piece*

The Experience

Sealed lips parted by moist tongues
Your neck hints of suckle while being exposed
Seeing blue in a dark star filled sky
We pause into confusing eyes
Blinded by brightness
From a graceful blinking of an eye
Equal tension crowds the sheets
A soft kiss on the forehead
Then we sleep

A Granted Wish

Wondering through the night
I dwell on secret passages
That forms the quest
Panting to the opening of your eyes
As they pose as open windows
To your near, but far inner voice
Shooting stars form a pathway
As I enter a realm
Touched by wishes granted

What I Want

The Goddess that worships the water
But praises the fire

Renewed Vows

Trying to avoid the rain
I run blindly into the storm
Enclosed
Nervous, naked, wondering
The sky roars
The clouds cry light
Finding comfort from the unusual
The unusual roars, the unusual cries
Captivated by the unexpected
Such as the roaring hawk, spiraling out of control
For the love, the survival, of the canary yellow Chic-a-Dee
Instinctively grasping the concept of purity
The blind man growing into vision
Walking the path of regenerated emotions
Received and returned
Enclosed in a box, thinking outside of
Shivering lips as if thunder and lightning
Have just kissed
Knowledge of why Zion exists
Screams for this to persist
I take the responsibility of blowing daily
The sweet butterfly a kiss
Grant my wish. Say yes
Before the question verbally exist

In My World

In my world rivers walk and mountains talk
Raindrops outline the path less traveled in my world
Storms glide through empty valleys in my world
Clouds form songs of freedom in my world
In my world a woman is a woman
Never gets treated like a girl
In my world

Give Me Kisses

If I'm around you, kiss me
If I'm gone, locate me and kiss me

Patience

I lay eyes closed
Hoping that you know
I care
Praying that you listen
To my heart
Knowing that
Having a starting date
Opens up the flood gate
For an ending in time
Knowing that
Falling in love with you
Physically and emotionally
As I have already done mentally
Will take many moons
To allow the flower to blossom, petal by petal
The sun must bow to the rain
To be selfish would be holding on to your smile
No honor would I have
For making your love mine
Awakening to the tap of patience

Decisions

I'm about to suffocate
But it's not like I can't breathe
I don't want you on top of me
Can't dare ask you to leave
I'm tangled in your hair
Even though your not here
Weird
The sun falls upon my back
There is no shadow here
Only whispers
With the proof that there is still sun to share
Shall I dare not to suffocate?

The Love Letter

From a distant glance polished off by a crooked smile
I had emptiness
For what I felt at that given moment
Running backwards while simultaneously leaping forward
Rapping my arms around
Gently, but firm
Letting go while positively holding on
With no ability of reassurance
As this breath in hailed seemed deeper than others
Passionate
Karma
Chilly in her presence
Luke warm fingertips strengthens unstable legs
Shivering firm
No regrets of the taken leap
Now running forward while moving backwards
Stepping one foot inside I reject the welcome
Silence for a while
Ignoring the knocks
Starring at the door
Stepping away wanting to step forward
Wanting my mind to want such as my heart
Indecisively she moves away from rejection
Outside of emptiness
With only the invasions of crooked smiles
Accompanied by the vision of distant glances
My flower is soon swept up by another gust of wind
Finding myself as a result denying myself
Trying to awaken
Winded after soulfully fighting to only defeat myself
Walking anonymously
I wonder upon a field of recall
Surprisingly the door it's here

Right here in front of me
The unexpected ringing of the phone
Brings sounds of encouragement
Arms open
Anticipating the chance to engulf the opportunity of yesterday
Striving with a fast pace only to move cautious
Cautiously chasing the idea of longevity
Answering the knock before the second
Entering while opening the door
Running forward while moving forward
Passionate
Karma

I Ask You….

Places I've been, people I've seen
Life travels, life occupants
Earth deeds gone badly
Asking for redemption
Sinking heads above water
Easy directions
Dead end streets
On Zion, in hell
Never, should I dwell
To little time
Giant hearts drops
On and on, never shall we stop

A Piece of Love…..

Flowers in December
Olives in wine
Rainbows in the rain

Yellow chocolate on a golden tray
Orange, Oranges
Unbelievable, so daily I pray

For You...

Apples of essence
Nurturing flames of future
Just cause...
Anxiety inside out
Non-knowing spectacles
Escape, inner barrier
Time maximum
Time minimal
Exhale.

Because I'm,

Many miles away
Obstacles easily leaped
Time, a matter of...
Hearts beat at parallel
Easy, no such thing
Roots... The purist

Forever....

Sweet pedals spinning in the wind
Innocently lifted from their stem
Silently drifting
Time... destined to catch up
Excitement, interacts the process
Reality reaches the root
Spring begins to flourish another sweet rose

My Daughter

*My self accomplishment
Is based on her birth
My daughter
She lives within me
Woven into my flesh
Her soul heals my wounds
As she waits for her vessel
To take her through
My tunnel of life*

Until the End of Time

Flowers swaying from left to right in the confused wind
Opened eyes, closed to sunlight
Rain gently taps the windowsill
Every breath counts…one, two
Vibration dictates surrounding sounds
Every breath counts …three, four
Rough winds calmed by nature's structure

Fires tamed by moist teardrops
Reflected rays from the moon, bounce off the ocean's surface
Individual identities commence into sync
Endless ocean waves tug against the under toe
Nighttime skies flip the atmosphere
Denial of a better day, dissolved with war
Stay in peace, stay in my heart forever

Because,

In your eyes, deep, I look into

Listen to the loudness of silence, loudly
Outer limits line the surface outwardly
Victory only in the heart, only in the soul
Even you, even I, yes even we

Yelling, in the silence of love making love
Otherwise, ice freezes the frost, once bitten
Understand my love lies in my eyes

Insight

We sometimes pause in life at a stumble in our emotional path. Creating obstacles that seem greater then they are. Stunned by this overwhelming conflict of the heart, we fold.

A Poem to the World
Blue sky
Gray clouds
Nature without oxygen
Lessons learned
Knowledge gained
Single souls
Marrying their neighbor's trust
Grasping the concept of unity
Many eyes, same focus
Locked hands creating a bond of enlightment
Bowed heads with moist cheeks
Rising to the glory of sunlight
There is a day, which will be better
Faith

Be Strong My Friend

Be strong my friend
Time never ends
'Til the soul gives in
Be strong my friend
You must go down before you win
Be strong my friend
Eyes wide!
Openly, the rainbow shines in
Be strong my friend
Firm!
Never bend with the wind

Lady Bug

At the opening of an eye
She sits firmly into my life
Her heart flutters
With the tempo of the wind
Disappearing at nightfall
Softly into secrecy
Returning in morning
With strong wings
Fluttering loudly,
Each stroke breaks the silence of the wind
Hurting my eardrums painlessly
Once again firmly fitting
I embrace the beauty
Of my disappearing lady bug

Caribbean Eyes

Once upon a time
Sweet scented clovers
Played in the wind
Gently, as two siblings
Silently, but out loud
Singing
Quietly
Gliding toward the sky
I can hear the message in the whistle
They sing so humble
They sing so happy
The song changes as they cross my path
I stare at them, as if they are a pair of eyes
Instantly
I realize
These are my Caribbean Eyes

Passion for Her

Passion for her…………………..Yes
Love for her……………………..Yes
Belief in her……………………..Yes

Strength so intoxicating
I am sucked in
Drawn into a life I cannot share
Only watch
Just watching
Doesn't work anymore
My blinding worth
Invisible to her eyes
Should I stay?
I will go blind

Your, Choice

I hate it when you lie to me
Although you look really cute doing it
I hate it when you argue with me
Although you know you shouldn't
I guess I wouldn't love you
If it was all good or all bad
Just remember
The next lie
The next argument
May be your last

    Love Always,
        Could be your past, could be your future.

Journey

The blinding light lay across the sky
Winds blew from every direction
Trees fell, Rocks rolled.
Even the old bell had a story to be told
I closed my eyes with a blinding sigh
I tried to climb, without the help of my eyes
Empty touches, as I moved with no sense of direction
The force of the wind, made me tighten my over-clothe again and again
If I give up now all will be forgotten
I must gather all my thoughts to reach the top of this mountain.
The struggle that I proceed to enter, is the struggle of all humanity
I wonder if the scientists know the length of this terrain.
Confusion held me back
So a promised religion I could never be attached.
I stayed my own person and kept an open mind
I heard that if you weren't a prisoner of your day in time
Ever lasting space wouldn't be hard to find
I thought, I wondered, but never could I find
This space full plane; which I could never grasp when I was alive.

You Decide:

A Conversation; between friends.

Perfect winds
Light sounds from empty cans of tin
Can you relate to my visions dear friend?
How about those leaves
Filled with the endless pigment of green within
Trash, trees
Opens my eyes to my destiny
This journey indeed may see me breathe
Perhaps take my last breath away from me
The reply-
Partners we may be
Never forgetting the first time you said what's up to me
I know not what you say you see
Me
Tin cans that outline many streets
Overfilled trash cans
More paper than leaves
Someday those brown leaves
Dehydrating trees
May one day breathe?
But not today
Nor in the near future
Me
I just can't see
The vision you pose to me
Now back to me-
As I listen to the words you say to me
Starring me in the eyes
As your screams turn into one big cry
My, my, my
With such intensity my dreams you deny
Clip my wings
Giving me reasons why I can't
Or shouldn't fly
My reach is longer than that of those you know

Those that extend to only the brim of that bucket
As I roll out of control
Landing on my back
Startled
But my shell it didn't crack
Motivation persist
Your voice in the back ground
Telling me to come back
The question-
Did you forget that you're black?
White trash
Mexican
 Perhaps Puerto Rican-
You must really want me to weaken
I'm what you would call human
Deaf ears your request falls upon
The courage to proceed
No longer will I hear you say I lack
Remembering that chant before the slaves
The one that kept empty souls brave
That chant that says life didn't start with these bad days
Gold cups filled with crushed grapes you would taste
Tender meat
Packed with endless spices upon every one's plate
You lifted with brass folks polished
Until they revealed your face
You have more than enough strength
To complete this walk
Hoping you realize the importance of this talk
One last time I'll invite you on this walk
Back to where we were-
Consistent, as you drill in my head
The woman was made in the image of you
A man
You're the flesh as she stands as the following shadow
A belief-
Without you she can't stand
Sinking teeth directed into fruit
That hints with a ripeness fresher than fine
Nose hairs rise

As an individual flower gives off the scent to covet the pedals of life
That single rose
Impacting far beyond the gathering of a bunch
Travels that seem lonely
Since the scarlet letter you bestowed upon me
That spirit that you believe you took
Instilled an inner faith
That made me proud to be that crab
That shook the grasp of your rusty hook
No animosity here as our bond disappears
Pass or fail
For me, shed no tears
To you old friend
Guidance and blessings
A few, not many words
But those would have heeled the deepest wounds
Your words made me endure
Knowledge is knowledgeable
So know the darkest fear I shall not fear
Without gills
I engulf the salt that lies purified in any ocean
Finless I'll cut through towering waves
Carried on backs of restless seas
Standing tall on bent knees
Perched on one foot
Balanced with the confidence of a four legged beast
Swimming up stream in a battered texture mudslide
Listen to my heart beat by focusing on my eyes
Feel my inner strength
Instilled from her inner strength
Gracefully passed on through her womb
Ending with the beginning-
Perfect winds, light sounds from empty cans of tin.
Hint
One foot forward assures the journey to never end

Insight

Happiness falls within the heart
As we chase the scent of suckle
Gasping for the full aroma of an atmosphere
That has already been touched by the gentle embrace of love

Through My Eyes

Do you see what I see?
Tall trees, filled with purple and pink leaves
Golden sunflowers filled with seeds
Do you see what I see?
Bluish green seas
The greenest of the green under me
Do you see what I see?
Orange and brown leaves
White clouds that say
"Come to me"
Do you see what I see?
Come let's see
I'll show you what I can see

10 Things I Did to Break Your Heart

1. As you whisper "I love you" in the depths of intimacy. From me no response

2. I cooked your favorite meal for someone other than you.

3. Gave you to them

4. Selfishly absorbed your emotions only not to reciprocate.

5. I said I wasn't ready for a relationship.

6. I embraced the other as if it was you

7. Emotionally said no when I verbally said yes

8. As you walked glidingly in my presence. I ignored your inner beauty

9. I said "I Love You"

10.......I walked away.

I inhale with only the purpose of...
Sipping your breath
Taste buds
Attentive
Whispering vibes nurtured through
The vision of certainty
Destitute of serenity
As if...
As if I pressed my lips upon your lips
Your lips would crumble
I wake up with disappointment
Wanting to sleep again
And again
To be closer to the thought
Further away from reality
Scared to smudge the crystal
I put my finger print
On the glass

One Thing I forgot to tell you…

I'm Sorry!

Cheating

Communication
Through the introduction of lips
Comforting
Such as the embrace of...
With the assistance of the pressing of two cheeks
You're not the one I chose
But your kiss makes me weak
Like a blink that puts me into next week
On that level
When of us I speak
One kiss and my kids
It makes me miss
Gracefully
I bow out of passion
Not to submit
Emotionally
Shall I be stoned?
If one kiss
One kiss
Can make me want to leave home

Forgiveness was offered and accepted
So much to let go of
So much to look forward to
Growth came in the blink of an eye
A friendship was mended all in due time
Boundaries set
Honest words have been spoken

                                        Thank You.

HER

My Soul aches for her
Many years has passed
Time does not heal all wounds
Her love is irreplaceable
Every tear I shed tells our story
Reality......SUCKS
I want a hug from her
I miss her
I miss..........her
Her touch
Her laughter
Her cry
The Honesty that lived in her eyes

"I want you to feel love. The way, I feel love. When you let me, love you".

C.R.P

From One to Another

Some say it's not right
But with all my might
I'm going to fight
Show you the light
The rainbow that shines bright
All through the night
It's a beautiful sight
So, I'll hold you tight
WHY?
'Cause it's a beautiful sky
I can see it in your eyes
It's written on your face
No surprise
Together we rise

The world is my grape. May I peel it?

That Feeling

I always wanted to see her
I just couldn't find the time
I always wanted to hold her
Technically she wasn't mine
I decided to take my chances
Ran my fingers through her hair
The feeling
One that only God could share
That feeling
To it I knew I would never be an heir
I began to comfort her each and everyday
Before I knew it
All I wanted to do was stay
One day
That feeling went away
It took all my energy and happily walked away

She called!

Through My Eyes (part II)

I ask you to see as me
Knowing that then
You will hold the key
Do you see what I see?
Nieve
Never once did I ask
Can I see what you see?
Together we planted seeds
Now they grow on opposite sides of the sea

?

No answers why
Only the memory of...
What was said to be
Questions with no purpose
Answers with no dialogue
Words without thinking
What has become of our love?

Flame

Laminated in ice
My soul glows
With the enlightenment of fire
Ocean walls pour upon my back
Never touching the fire that burns
Simply because the flame
Eternally burns in my heart

Star Gazing
(Dedication to a friend)

Stars hover over
Circles with sharp edges
Emptiness beyond bounds
STRANGE?!
Endless fantasies
On my back, my knees, my feet
Timeless segments of intrigue
ZONIN'!
Looking for a place to land
Flowers of beauty, blossoming in the sand
Waterfalls of frozen raindrops
Perfect as it may be
I wonder one day, will it really lay on top of me?
Taking it all away, my soul, my heart
I wonder as I star gaze?

As We Lay

Butterflies kiss
Waves overlap waves
Palm trees persuaded to sway
The moon divides night from day
As we lay

Injected

Injected by the unseen
Ejected by what society would think of me
Pain unbelievable pain
My poor love box
She is yelling at me
No she is screaming at me
Holding me hostage
As I scream help me
I invited the unseen
Welcomed it into my secret garden
Opened wide
I didn't know
My poor garden
Flowers wither
Butterflies painted in a childish manner
Sit with shades of black and white
Wings to heavy to fly
As the humming of the bees fade
How will my garden grow?

Your Touch

Sitting alone in the darkness
I savior the memory of your touch
Like fresh peeled grapes still on the vine
I indulge in the fruitful experience
Taking full advantage of opportunity
Holding on lightly
With the grip of finger tips
Your touch
As calming as a gentle kiss
That, touch
I miss

A Whole Half

I stand as a complete half
Shifting in the grace of instinct
Pacing to the beat of the drum
Seeking vision from faith
Unbalanced on the rope of future
Posing for the other half
The sealing that makes the soul authentic
I stand incomplete
Waiting for the last touch
The gloss

Tears

The cup overflows
Misdirecting the stream that flows upward
Every drop that finds salvation through evaporation
Is replaced by another drop from the backward flow
At last, the overflowing cup
Has ceased to shed another
Recognizing the first drop
Emerged from the blinking of a weeping eye
That once vision love

Sleepless Nights

My eyes are closed
My mind...open
With visions of your grace
Comfortable on a bed of gold
Unlimited riches when visualizing your face
Sleepless nights
With no tosses or turns
Sleepless nights
In the comfort of the night
Timeless thoughts
Who would have thought?
Enjoying sunshine
That the night has brought

*I found love
In a room full of lust
Put into the position of trust
Taken out of the situation of loneliness
Instantly
Taken out of being just me
Put into me
Loving
Caring
Romantic me
I lost me into her
Fogged windows becomes clear
Come…
I wish she was here*

The Question

Dimmed lights shine overhead
Opposite of absence tells the untold story
Timeless, overwhelmingly confusing
Outer surface, fragile as fresh snowflakes
Yellow inner soul brightness beyond imagination
Am I in love?

Now I Know Love

You open our hearts like four walls gasping for air
Letting in those of the unknown attractions
You allow the song to sing, as loudly as permitted by
one self
We dance as joyful as we wish
You show tears that seem to be endless
Heartaches that feel timeless
You give us unlimited time to recognize that there is not
enough time
You disappear
You watch us stumble
Whispering in the wind for us to calm down
You say you will soon come again
We wait, we listen, we anticipate
Realizing that the light we desire
The food for soul we hunger for has yet to flourish
inside
No longer searching for you
I see you inside me now
Now I know love

Is It Possible?

How do I tell her, that special someone that I love, "I Love you"? While saying "I'm not going to be there". Not going anywhere far, just not able to be there. You know. There on that walk. Walking close enough to the ocean to feel the moistness in the sand. There in that conversation when she laughs at all my jokes and I look her in the eyes and say to myself. "Only if you knew how much I Love you". As she smiles and asks me what I'm thinking. "Tell me" she says with a witty smile. Reminding me, about not keeping secrets. Maybe not being there for those bad days. The days that she refuses to move in the morning because her head hurts and she won't be able to function until she gets not only an aspirin, but also a head massage. "While you're at it, you might as well do my back". She chuckles out. How do I not be there? That one day she comes home and says "I had a great day." Inviting me, to listen, as she glows with excitement. So eager to put me in those places of her day, to share her smiles. How do I not be there? Listening. Knowing that the song she sings is only for my ears. Tell me. How does the rain turn its back on the nurturing tree? The sun saying "No, I will not be there". To the expecting dawn. Tomorrow telling today that today will be the last day. Tell me how do I be the thorn on that rose?

Forgiveness

I made you cry
Silent when you asked me why
Stunned by my own disgrace
To say sorry is not enough
To say I never meant to hurt you
Is not near tough
I ask for forgiveness
Not to seek forgetfulness
"The world" would I say
If you ask me "what I miss"
A thousand sorrows to match
A quarter of every tear
I love you and I truly hold
You & your heart dear

Closed Eyes/Time to Fly

Closed eyes
Sleeping for decades
A sweet aroma
Comforts the day
Relaxed to the norm
We stay
Rhythms send vibrations
Releasing tension of the day
Closed eyes
Opens half-way
One night, decides I pray
Images of flying
Wings spread as wide as the day
A sign
So I know, now it's okay
No-more dark days
Closed eyes
Now not afraid
Closed eyes
Now opened wide
Now I see
Opened eyes not afraid to fly
Ask me why?

Rainy Days

Visions of sandy Nile valleys
Orange dust floats
As it outlines the image of rage
I cry dreaming of rainy days
As the cattle rise to graze
I cry dreaming of rainy days
Petal by petal flowers begin to unfold
Once again the sleeping wishes their story to be told
Fresh fruit picked from its vine
Lustful more so than a fine new dime
The sun says no
I shine... it's my time
All hands fold, all faces cold
As I cry for rainy days

Distant Lover

Quick images
Lasting momentarily
Illusions of pictures painted in my dreams
As I laid holding your image
Your scent
Your creation
In my arms
Waking to see in reality
Them who were not you
Closing my eyes hesitating to open them
Hoping that it was you
Hoping that she was you
Constantly thinking of you
You
My distant lover
I stand arms opened
Waiting for you
Wanting for you
Unexpectingly the wind blew
It was you
My distant lover

EVOL

Listen to my heart
I can feel the warmth
As your head lies on my chest
Touching your lips
Touching my lips
Passion begins to mist
Placing all of me
Inside all of you
I feel at home now
Comfortable in your presence
I feel your blanket of assurance
Over lap what the night has brought
Does your love parallel mine?
Does my love overflow yours?
Love unlimited
Love undermined
May I cherish tonight all night?
Perfect, but verbally say, "It's not right."
Hold on to thee
Solid, strong, deeply rooted
Implanted as a seed
Now meant to be as a family tree

Join Love

You say you love
But have yet to allow love to grow
To grow deep inside the heart
You allow emotions to carry the weight of lust
You decide on reflected winds
You love without loving
Surfing on unbalanced vibes
Join the blessing of love making
Join the world in love knowing
Join love

Sunflower

As a lonely sunflower in the breeze
I sit in the courtyard alone
Like the soft touch of a bee
As it lands gently upon a petal
I wait with patience for you presence
Overwhelmed by charisma
I embrace the aura of comfort
Letting go of all else
For the sunflower is wild.

Fate

We emerge in thoughts
Imagining the future we desire
Placing labels on items of forever
Erasing all exploration dates
Hold my hand
Walk with me
Let's go through what our souls already knew
It was fate

Is IT Possible?
(Part 2)

Is it possible to love and hurt at the same time?
A rage, impossible to control.
At this point I am just trying to let go
Gain control
Hoping for release
As I breathe in deep
Hoping to release her as I exhale
But she only moves deeper into me
Into my soul
A parasite relationship
But who is feeding
Her or me
Maybe both
Our hungers are opposite
So must be what nourishes us

Reality

Tension vibrates the motion
Rotating the soul's balance
Bareness
Dresses the once clothed
Falling mist combines identity
Wetness,
Quenches all threats of dehydration
Balance
Assures the stability of emotion
Nature
Permits the cycle to circle

Soaring Angel/Once Fallen

I float through
The gates of gravity
As if
An angel
Searching
Reaching for my wingspan
The spin is steady
As released tension
Reveals itself
Screaming
For the time has come to relax
The volume of silence
Turned down
By the hands of calmness
I hear the melody
In tune with the rhyme
Courage
Curiosity
Soaring to the ends of time

Insight

To have thoughts unfolding, in mind, is to be the bulb. Growing, unfolding, into something beautiful. A flower.

Dear you,

It was nice to hear from you after all this time. So many things have changed since we were one. The echoes of your voice in my memories of us brought back a lot of those vibes that we use to hum along side of. Remembering that day, those days, all those roads we've paved. Acting crazy laughing, crying. I can still hear you sighing. Not for nothing, I know you're going to think I'm lying. However that idea about your hair, I did care. Oh, about that bike I didn't need. I got it. It fits me! If I'm babbling, please forgive me. I never took the time out to write me. Or should I say write my better half. You always did have a special way to make me laugh. I've always been thankful for the time we've shared. You know, it's funny that so many people live their lives without finding that unique individual. That individual that freely allows them to experience, the experience, of experiencing themselves; while embracing another. And that, that's you. So with that, I'm thankful to you for being the nourishment that permits me to grow into myself daily.

Love me,
Love You.
The Exit

I haven't learned how to swim,
But luckily I've learned how to tread water.

Wishful Thinking

I wish I could see what you see when you look at me
Maybe point out my insecurities
That I refuse to see
I wonder if you wish for me
To humble the lion within me
Straining my eyes, hoping to see
What it is that you see?
Is my stroke to firm?
To caress your silky hair
Are my hands to rough?
To touch your smooth Skin
As I look at you
I cry
To know your thoughts within
Hoping to know answers
That will allow me in...
Your heart
Your mind
Your soul
But until then
I wish I could see what you see
When you look at me
For it seems forever you're apart of me

Solid Confusion

Seeing truly for the first time
How bad love really hurts
As you collapse in my arms
I feel hollow inside
Not knowing how to resolve your pain
Your tears shatter against my skin
That sits uncovered soaking up your memories
Carried away through your tears
Wanting to give you everything
In this world twice
I'm settled
With an embrace and hopes of your fulfillment
In my arms
Confused about my feelings
Do I hold these emotions for you?
Or perhaps your sorrows
Knowing it's not enough
I squeeze a little bit tighter.

The Beauty Darkness Brings

As I inhale the deepest breathe I have ever taken
My eyes rest at peace
Sealing all light that may attempt to shed darkness
On the light that lies on the other side of my vision
It lay very strategic, as it flowed
Steady
Creamy
Like caramel dripping
Flowing gracefully from its core
Tarnished by only beauty
Deep
Solid
Smooth
Beauty
Like that first tear drop hinted of salt
Willingly falling to the tip of a tongue
Beauty
That embrace so tight one wish to squeeze tighter
In the hopes of the two, becoming one
Beauty
As I stare at you
Wondering how you can make silk look so good as it gowns you
Beauty
Like every time I close my eyes I think of you
Beauty… like that

A Letter Not a Poem

From my finger tips
To the tip of my toes
I feel a chill in my soul
Shivering
I stare into emptiness
Visualizing the heat that's not there
I lean over
Striking a match
Lighting a candle
Your candle
The plush candle
With the slightly tilted leaf
Its rose colored veins deeply engraved
Clinching my hands
Starring into the flame
Feeling the heat
Remembering the heat
Confused
Confused about my fate
Starring at the source of the heat
Wondering why?
Why hasn't it reached me?
Like a first grade student
On the first day of school
I wait for questions
To seek answers
Wanting to ask questions of know how
So I can know how
How to feel more
More than the reflections beyond the flame

It's cold
I'm cold
I feel your cold hands
I feel as if am connected to your soul
I miss you
I miss us
I wish you serenity
I wish you shed not a tear
I wish I could be right there
Filling that void
Avoiding the lashes of heartache
One hand hurts
The other just wants to shake
So cold
So the candle I blow out
Freezing the only remembrance of your warmth

While I'm down here on one knee, I was wondering…

…"Will you marry me?"

Author's Image:

*"To paint a self-portrait of myself,
Would only put me on a higher shelf. So I'll leave it up
to you to decide, the image of my self pride".
Caros R. Pendleton*

www.ingramcontent.com/pod-product-compliance
Lightning Source LLC
Chambersburg PA
CBHW031408040426
42444CB00005B/469